X-treme DISASTERS
THAT CHANGED AMERICA

WILDFIRE!

The 1871 Peshtigo Firestorm

by Jacqueline A. Ball

Consultant: Daniel H. Franck, Ph.D.

BEARPORT
PUBLISHING COMPANY, INC.

New York, New York

Credits

Cover, Bill Stormont/CORBIS, National Park Service, Wisconsin Historical Society.

Title page, Wisconsin Historical Society; Page 4-5, Wisconsin Historical Society; 6, Danny Lehman / Corbis; 7, W. Perry Conway / Corbis; 8-9, National Park Service; 10-11, Wisconsin Historical Society; 12, 13, Mike Gora; 14-15, 16, Wisconsin Historical Society; 18, Louis Pappas and Monica Ponomarev; 19, National Park Service; 20, Corbis; 21, Wisconsin Historical Society; 22-23, Library of Congress Prints & Photographs Collection; 24-25, Clyde H Smith / Getty Images; 25, Mike McMillan / Spotfire Images; 26, James P. Rowan / rowanpix.com; 27, The Peshtigo Times; 29, Raymond Gehman / Corbis.

Design and production by Dawn Beard Creative, Triesta Hall of Blu-Design, and Octavo Design and Production, Inc.

Library of Congress Cataloging-in-Publication Data

Ball, Jacqueline A.
  Wildfire! : the 1871 Peshtigo firestorm / by Jacqueline A. Ball ; consultant, Daniel H. Franck.
      p. cm. — (X-treme disasters that changed America)
  Includes bibliographical references and index.
  ISBN 1-59716-011-3 (lib. bdg.)—ISBN 1-59716-034-2 (pbk.)
  1. Forest fires—Wisconsin—Peshtigo Region—History—19th century—Juvenile literature.
  2. Peshtigo Region (Wis.)—History—19th century—Juvenile literature. I. Title. II. Series.

  SD421.32.W6B25 2005
  363.37'9—dc22

                          2004020747

For more information, write to Bearport Publishing Company, Inc., 101 Fifth Avenue, Suite 6R, New York, New York 10003. Printed in the United States of America.

3 4 5 6 7 8 9 10

Table of Contents

An Orange Glow 4

Disaster in the Making 6

Deadly Wind 8

Get to the River! 10

Safe on Green Island. 12

"The Saddest City in the World" 14

Nothing but Ashes 16

Dry and Dangerous 18

Scarred for Life 20

Was It a Comet? 22

Can We Prevent Another Wildfire? 24

Peshtigo Today 26

Just the Facts 28

Glossary 30

Bibliography 31

Read More. 31

Learn More Online 31

Index 32

About the Author. 32

An Orange Glow

Green Island Lighthouse keeper Mary Drew looked across the bay. The still, smoky air made her eyes water. The smoke had hung in the air for weeks. Ships out on Lake Michigan sounded their foghorns because the smoke was so thick. In Green Bay, a part of the lake, the Green Island Light was on day and night.

Mary saw an orange glow across the bay. It was coming from Peshtigo (PESH-tuh-go), Wisconsin. A puff of wind blew in her face. Then the wind blew harder. It was Sunday, October 8, 1871. The deadliest wildfire in United States history was beginning.

▼ An aerial view of Peshtigo before the fire

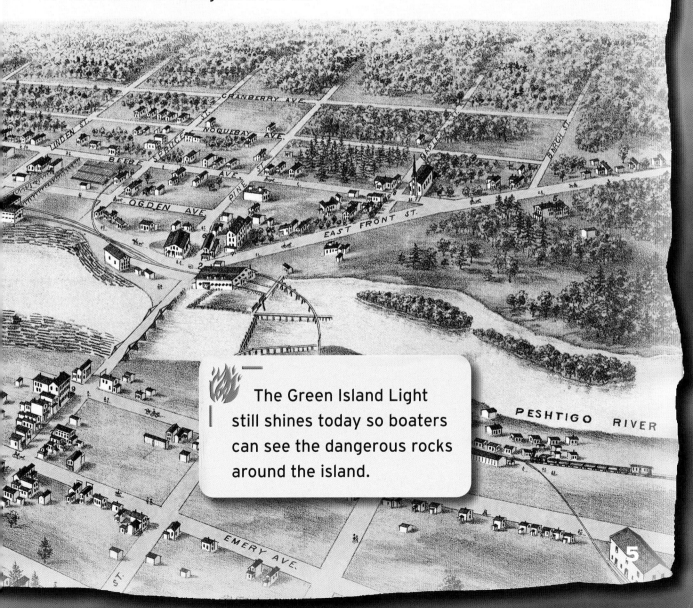

The Green Island Light still shines today so boaters can see the dangerous rocks around the island.

5

Disaster in the Making

Peshtigo was a **lumber** town. Many **loggers** worked in the nearby forest. They left behind huge piles of branches, twigs, and leaves. This waste was called slash.

▲ Smoke from slash and burn in Panama

Piling up slash and then setting it on fire is called "slash and burn."

Often, hunters left their campfires burning, and the slash caught fire. Sometimes sparks flew from trains and started fires, too. These small fires didn't usually spread. People didn't worry about them. Sometimes they set the fires on purpose to clear the land.

The weather that summer in Peshtigo was unusual. It was very hot and had rained only two times. Many small fires filled the woods and thick smoke hung over the forest.

▲ An example of slash and burn in Peru

Deadly Wind

On October 8, a blast of cold air blew in from the West. When it hit the still, warm air over Wisconsin, it caused a strong windstorm. The wind made the small fires become bigger.

The wind howled. It caused the fire to spin into giant flaming wheels. The fire wheels traveled from tree to tree.

In Peshtigo, white flakes began to fall. They looked like snowflakes, but they were really ashes. They were deadly signs that the fire was on its way. Then a 100-foot wall of fire moved out of the forest like a **hurricane**.

▼ This forest fire spread quickly, just like the one in Peshtigo.

Some people say the wind was 300 miles per hour—over three times faster than the winds of most hurricanes.

Get to the River!

The fire hit Peshtigo like a bomb exploding. Flames ate up homes, schools, and other buildings. The fire was so hot it boiled water in wells. The wind tossed houses and railroad cars into the air.

▼ **Picture of the fire in Peshtigo from Nov. 25, 1871, edition of _Harper's Weekly Magazine_**

Screaming people raced through town. Their hair and clothes were burning. Hundreds jumped into rivers and streams. Scared cattle ran in after them, crushing people under their hooves.

Due to the heat, people could only keep their heads above water for a few seconds at a time. Some drowned and others were hurt or killed when flaming branches fell on them.

Reports say the fire was 1,500°F to 2,000°F. The fire was so hot it could have melted steel.

Safe on Green Island

On Green Island, red-hot ashes fell on the wooden buildings. Mary Drew's children rushed to throw water on them.

The winds turned the water around the island into wild waves. Suddenly, a boat crashed onto the rocks. Mary's husband hurried to save the crew.

Mary climbed the tower to tend to the light. From up there, the whole shore glowed red. About an hour later, the wind changed. As a cold rain began to fall, steam rose from the burning ground.

The Drews and the crew were lucky. They were safe and the buildings were still standing.

▶ Green Island (in background)

Peshtigo couldn't ask other towns for help because the **telegraph** wires had burned.

▲ Green Island Lighthouse after the fire

"The Saddest City in the World"

The next morning, the Drews looked out at a different world. The shore was a pile of black **rubble**. Floating wood and black ash covered the bay.

Only one building in Peshtigo was standing. It was surrounded by a large clearing that kept the fire away.

Across the water, Peshtigo had been wiped out. Eight hundred people, half the city, had died. Every horse, cow, dog, sheep, pig, and chicken was killed. The fire had been so hot it turned humans and animals to ashes.

Peshtigo had truly gone up in smoke. A newspaper even called it "the saddest city in the world."

▼ **A building destroyed by the fire in Peshtigo.**

Nothing but Ashes

The firestorm raced through Wisconsin and parts of Michigan. It flattened twelve other towns and over a million acres of wood. In total, an area twice the size of Rhode Island was lost.

Many stories say between 1,200 and 1,700 people died. Some say more than 2,000 died. No one knows the real number of deaths. Birth records were burned up in the fire. Often there was nothing left of a body to **identify**.

▲ People fleeing the Great Peshtigo Fire

Peshtigo lost more people and **property** than any other town. For this reason, the disaster is known as the Great Peshtigo Fire.

A wildfire is another name for a forest fire. A firestorm is a wildfire with winds of at least 90 miles per hour.

Dry and Dangerous

Many believed the fire started for two reasons. First, people were not careful. **Brush** fires were set to clear land. People usually let the fires burn without watching them. Second, there was a **drought**. The heat dried out **wetlands** and made evergreen trees lose their needles. The dry needles caught fire. Then the sudden wind turned the forest into a fireplace.

Firestorm!

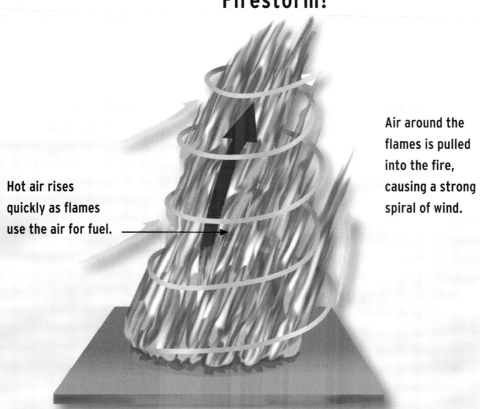

Hot air rises quickly as flames use the air for fuel.

Air around the flames is pulled into the fire, causing a strong spiral of wind.

Forest fires heat the air. The heated air rises and draws in the surrounding cold air. The cold air, which begins to spin, becomes fuel for the flames as they rise higher and higher. Soon the flames rush through the forest in a flash.

After the fire started, the town was in trouble. Buildings were made of wood. Sawdust covered floors of mills and stores. Around Peshtigo, creeks and marshes were very dry. Peshtigo was food for the hungry flames.

◀ A forest fire in Yellowstone National Park in 1988

The first cause of forest fires is people not being careful. Lightning is the second cause of forest fires.

Scarred for Life

In the morning, people crept through their **destroyed** town. Most were badly burned. Some had broken bones and a few had gone blind from the fire's heat.

Their suffering was not over. Their families were gone. They had no place to go because their homes had been burnt down. There was nothing to eat because there were no more animals or **crops**.

Staying in the water had saved most people's lives. Others lived because they had buried themselves in the sand. They would have terrible **scars** on their faces, heads, and bodies for the rest of their lives.

▲ After the fire in Peshtigo

The mix of wind and other conditions that caused the fire is known as the "Peshtigo Effect." This effect was studied to make firebombs during World War II.

Was It a Comet?

While Peshtigo dug out of the ashes, Chicago, Illinois, was doing the same thing. The Great Chicago Fire of 1871 started at the same hour on the same day. It killed 200 to 300 people and left 100,000 without homes.

Not far away, a third fire struck Holland, Michigan. Could three huge fires on one day, in the same area, have been an accident? Some people, including a scientist named Robert Wood, say maybe not. Wood says pieces of a **comet** named Biela (BEE-la) crashed near Lake Michigan and started the fires. Some don't agree with Wood. Others think he's right.

◀ Great Chicago Fire, 1871

National Fire Prevention Week is held in October because of the Great Chicago Fire.

Can We Prevent Another Wildfire?

People cause most forest fires. We can't stop the other ones, but we can keep them from becoming disasters.

Brush, for example, should be burned only when the forest is not too dry or windy. The fire should be kept small and watched carefully.

Once a wildfire starts, firefighters can use an airplane to dump water or chemicals on the blaze. They can also clear trees from around the fire with bulldozers. **Smokejumpers** can parachute into forests to fight fires on foot.

There are more than 100,000 forest fires each year in the United States.

Peshtigo Today

The terrible fire brought some good changes. Loggers no longer leave as much tree waste behind. **Improvements** have been made both in stopping fires from happening and in fire fighting. People now understand that they need to be careful about fires in the forest.

The Peshtigo Fire Museum building was once a church. People who died in the fire are buried outside.

The "saddest city in the world" has become "the city reborn from ashes." People who lived through the fire came back to rebuild their town. Mary Drew's son, Frank, grew up to be the lighthouse keeper on Green Island. Today, thousands visit the Peshtigo Fire Museum every year.

▲ Mrs. Amelia Desrochers survived the fire in Peshtigo.

Just the Facts

The 1871 Peshtigo Firestorm

- Many of the people who jumped in the river still died because there was no oxygen in the air. The fire had used it up.
- Some people thought the world was ending. They didn't even try to escape from the fire.
- Twenty-six years later, the forest was still not the same as it was before the fire.

Some of the worst wildfires in the United States

- **1881: Thumb Fire in Michigan**—This fire destroyed a million acres of land. It killed more than 250 people.
- **1894: Hinckley Fire in Minnesota**—This fire destroyed 160,000 acres of land. Over 400 people died.
- **1910: The Great Fire of 1910**—This fire destroyed about 3 million acres of land in Idaho and Montana and killed 86 people.

Fire Safety Improvements

- Better government programs have been set up to manage forests.
- Loggers get rid of slash more carefully.
- New tools and improved ways of fighting fires have been developed.

▲ A forest fire in New Mexico

Glossary

brush (BRUHSH)   an area of land where small trees and bushes grow

comet (KOM-it)   a bright heavenly body with a long cloudy tail of light

crops (KROPS)   plants that are grown and gathered, often for food

destroyed (di-STROID)   ruined completely

drought (drout)   a long period of dry weather

hurricane (HUR-uh-*kane*)   a storm with very high winds and heavy rain

identify (eye-DEN-tuh-fye)   to tell who someone is

improvements (im-PROOV-muhnts)   changes that make something better

loggers (LOG-urz)   workers who cut down trees

lumber (LUHM-bur)   timber or logs that have been sawed

property (PROP-ur-tee)   something that is owned, such as buildings and land

rubble (RUHB-uhl)   rough broken stones or bricks

scars (SKARZ)   marks left on the skin by a cut or burn

smokejumpers (SMOKE-*juhm*-purz)   firefighters who drop by parachute into a forest fire

telegraph (TEL-uh-*graf*)   a way to send messages over long distances using a code of electric signals

wetlands (WET-*landz*)   marshy lands; land where the soil is very moist or wet

Bibliography

House, Charles. "This Date in 1871, Peshtigo Killed 1,700." *The Milwaukee Sentinel.* October 8, 1953.

Leschak, Peter M. *Ghosts of the Fireground: Echoes of the Great Peshtigo Fire and the Calling of a Wildland Firefighter.* San Francisco, CA: Harper San Francisco (2002).

Read More

Liebig, Nelda Johnson. *Carrie and the Apple Pie.* Midwest Traditions (1999).

Liebig, Nelda Johnson. *Carrie and the Crazy Quilt.* Midwest Traditions (1996).

Vogel, Carole Garbuny. *Nature's Fury: Eyewitness Reports of Natural Disasters.* New York, NY: Scholastic (2000).

Learn More Online

Visit these Web sites to learn about the Peshtigo Fire and wildfires:

- http://www.nifc.gov/information.html
- http://www.peshtigofire.info

Index

ash
9, 12, 14-15, 16, 22, 27

brush fires
18

Chicago, Illinois
22

comet
22-23

Desrochers, Amelia
27

Drew, Mary
4-5, 12, 27

firefighters
25

firestorm
16-17, 18, 28

forest fires
9, 17, 18-19, 24-25, 29

Great Chicago Fire of 1871
22-23

Great Fire of 1910
28

Great Peshtigo Fire
16-17

Green Bay
4

Green Island
4, 12-13, 27

Green Island Light
4-5

heat
11, 18, 20

Hinckley Fire
28

Holland, Michigan
23

hurricane
9

Lake Michigan
4, 23

lightning
19

loggers
6, 26, 29

map
17

Michigan
16, 23, 28

Minnesota
28

National Fire Prevention Week
23

New Mexico
29

Panama
6

Peru
7

Peshtigo
5, 6-7, 9, 10-11, 12, 14-15, 17, 19, 21, 22, 26-27

Peshtigo Effect
21

Peshtigo Fire Museum
26-27

slash and burn
6-7

smokejumpers
25

Thumb Fire
28

wildfire
5, 17, 24-25, 28

wind
5, 8-9, 10, 12, 17, 18, 21, 24

windstorm
8

Wisconsin
5, 8, 16

Wood, Robert
23

Yellowstone National Park
19

About the Author

Jacqueline A. Ball has written and produced more than one hundred books for kids and adults. She lives in New York City and Old Lyme, Connecticut.